AVENUE OF ESCAPE

For Tsering
with best
wishes in
the Naropa
Ram —
Lewis [illegible]
7/95

Other Books by Lewis Warsh

The Suicide Rates
Highjacking
Moving Through Air
Chicago
Dreaming as One
Long Distance
Part of my History
Immediate Surrounding
Today
The Maharajah's Son
Blue Heaven
Hives
Methods of Birth Control
Agnes & Sally
The Corset
Information from the Surface of Venus
A Free Man

Lewis Warsh

AVENUE OF ESCAPE

LONG NEWS BOOKS
New York
1995

Some of these poems first appeared in *The American Poetry Review, Broadway, Transfer, Talisman, Cover, United Artists, Shiny, Notus, Southpaw, Out of This World* (Crown, 1992), *The World, Downtown Brooklyn, Poetry New York, From the Other Side of the Century* (Sun & Moon, 1994), and *Long News in the Short Century.*

Special thanks to Barbara Henning and Bill Kushner.

Cover by Yvonne Jacquette

Library of Congress: 95-75994
ISBN: 0-9645591-0-2

Long News Books, P.O. Box 150-455, Brooklyn, New York 11215

TABLE OF CONTENTS

for Wang Ping

TRAVELOGUE

To merely uncover the depths of love
By sitting here same spot establishes dignity
No more submissive than he was to his mother
A love forgotten but the lover's body remains
A ring of pure light circles the earth every hour
The point from which you begin to distort what you're trying
    to say
My imaginary brother follows me like a shadow
The woman upstairs says she thinks her dog found something that
    resembles a gerbil & ate it
Nietzsche was fun to read in prison
You can't love something that doesn't exist
The church, family, a tree whose branches fell off in the storm
No one will punish you if you feel too much pleasure
It's not cold outside but inside—it's like winter
What I saw when I looked down at the woman & her lover
    was a reflection of the shadow of the heart broken
    into shards
The agency of the letter moves through the fabric of fate
I had a crush on my neighbor but she moved out of town
The dress is made of cotton—it's really a jumper
How to hold a stranger at arm's length & comfort him?
The strangest part was when there was no place to go,
    no home, & I had to sit on stoops, out-doors,
    or loiter in shops, linger in restaurants over glasses
    of iced coffee & mint tea
Unable to speak the language of the Cantonese waitress
    whose job was "off the books" & whose livelihood
    depended on the amount of money I tipped her
Everything derives from a lack of attention, broken span

into which something drops
Depending on the day of the week or your mother I love you,
hate you more some days
I stand on the edge of town, light burning in the window
I drive through hopeless Canada, aching with dignity
I walk into the bodega & buy a lightbulb & a loose cigarette
A transparency of hair catches the flame of his first desire
They met in 1965 & lived together 4 years
Dark hallway filled with guys I don't know, smoking
I've saved some dinner, all I have to do is heat it up
When she returns from her job she neither kisses me nor says
hello
The people who cut through the fog with scythes went
on strike
Desire overcomes inertia, but the stones survive

THE OUTER BANKS

You could say that characters in The Bible were obsessed
with hiding their nakedness

I touch the leg of the table with the toe of my foot

The child searches in a drawer for the damaged toy

Feelings of love were impaired by excessive anxiety

I put in my order with the butcher before it gets too late
& the holidays are "upon us" or so they say

You can wear the same clothing every day & no one cares

She complains that she spends too much time making herself
beautiful while he just picks up the clothing he
wore yesterday from the floor & doesn't even
bother washing his face or combing his hair

I hear a rooster cry at dawn from someone's roof

I experience an epiphany, I'm not what you might call handy

There's a dead seal on the beach & a fishing boat
on the horizon

The guy downstairs complains about a leak when I take a
shower

Some people don't mind if you take them for granted

She can’t break up with her boyfriend until she knows
she has another waiting in the wings

It’s hard to love anyone who holds a grudge

I wear my compromises over my mask

My deficiencies won’t add up, no ice no drink

The shades of night toss their dilapidated forms over my
shoulders like a Ukrainian shawl

Women with kerchiefs, a family with stroller, her equestrian
thoughts ride into the sunset

Think of A’s love for B in terms of the needs of A for whom
B provides the promise of immediate gratification

The sun goes down in my mirror where I address myself not as
"I" but as a you who exists outside me & can’t think

I thought I’d take time out from my work to make a call
but as soon as I heard her voice I hung up

A 16-year old student has been charged as an adult with
attempted murder & unlawful use of a weapon in the
shooting of a teacher who ordered him to stop smoking

Seek out a stranger to alleviate desire but don’t call her
back—she might be "busy tonight"

It seems like you might as well have a drink to loosen you up

In the summer of 1964 I lived in a bungalow in Far Rockaway
with my girlfriend, her father & her baby

"She's not here now—she's never here—who should I say
called?"

It strikes me: it strikes me that I repeat everything twice in
my life, & keep repeating, without acknowledging my
mistakes

Some people keep love at a distance because they're frightened of
being hurt but it's hard to be on the outside looking in at
your own life or perpetually standing on the edge of
things with no where to go

We thought the matinee began at 3 but when we arrived it was
intermission

People meet on a blind date & eventually get married for the sake
of discretion ("my parents wanted me to")

You find out what interests you, but don't do it—not yet,
anyway—since it's more interesting to put it all off
till tomorrow, to let things slide, to trap the thought
in its beauty like a tiger in a cage & watch it climb the
walls & disfigure itself out of sheer helplessness

You map out a theory of knowledge & watch it dissolve like an
integer divided by itself, but turned on their sides
the numbers look like songs

You pretend to work hard so others will leave you alone

You talk to strangers & megalomaniacs, you read books you
read before

You prefer pieces of paper with words on them to people, but
that phase passes

You identify with the tree outside your window: all my family
makes a home here but the branches are obscure, even
to me

You sing a judicious symphony like a necklace of amber beads

A half-dressed man leans out the window & shouts to his
girlfriend on the sidewalk

A police car with a loud speaker announces a reward for any
information leading to the arrest & conviction of a person
who shot a policeman

I was working in the library at Columbia University & we met
during my lunch hour on the steps of Grant's Tomb

Tumblers on the tray bisect the light of the immigrant wafer
which we place on the tongue to taste the snow, the rain
& the spray which from yonder fountain alights on our
faces

There's a bracelet close to her skin that resembles ivy but if
I touch it I fear my heart might grow numb

The specialty of the house wasn't on the menu but you could
request it from the waiter, waitress or maitre d' who
would bow down & kiss your knees out of a desire to
give pleasure

Love is no solution to fear, the touch of a hand in the dark,
nor the flowers, nor the beating of the wings against
the screen

A job that represses your sexual instincts may be just what
you need

"Don't wait up for me" is something I might have said
but when I returned the bed was a talisman
of crumbs & plaster

They say there was a lot of rain & possible flooding before
we came: they tell us we brought the bad weather with us

Tell us what remains of desire, as you know it

All the swings in the park are taken, all the benches broken,
let's sit here

There's a jail across the border where they'll take us when
we get out of hand & from which we can see the evening
star, a symbol of the persistence of desire

All they can do is torture us, behold us in wonder at our
beauty, desiring to subjugate us because we're so unlike
them in our sweet ways, & even our most muddled
intuitions are wiser than the vows of militancy they
concoct

I go to the prison of the practical world to take care of
business

I look up my name in the index but it isn't listed

She was born & died before my time but if she were alive
today we might have been pals

Bodies intermingle in a subway car—I stare covertly at legs,
arms, eyes

I collect the wood & light the coals, but the wood is wet & I
have to use a whole box of blue tips just to keep
it going

I plant the symbol of order, Neptune's trident, on the opposite
side of the archipelago & set forth under warm skies to a
new terrain, spellbound by the possibilities of the future
& the shadows of the strange birds hanging motionless
on the horizon, but I don't know the name of the boat
I'm aboard—it's like a shadow of some other boat
that went down in the storm off the Isle of Good Hope,
where promises of love were made only to be broken
the next day, where marriage vows were spoken
in the shadows of an empty cathedral, where friends
& relatives gathered to wish you well—could
anyone of them, or you, predict
this spell of cold weather
we've been having recently?

All the objects in the world won't unlock the door to the
present where daylight strips us of night's desire
& a voice riding the airwaves whispers into the fog:
Don't lose heart

When I close my eyes I can see the after-image of the light
of the candle like the face in a dream, you are my
shadow

SISTER AGATHA'S LAMENT

You can't narrow it down to what matters, because it's too easy to say "nothing does" and that the sky may be clear but the cold seeps efficaciously through the cracks in the soul's armament giving us something to talk about other than what it feels like to be alive. Easy, too, to say that people are swallowed up by the objects they need, or that the things we produce determine the people we love. All I know is that something forbidden is desired: the guy who carts his groceries down the street in a wheelchair, the woman who calls someone else's child "honey," the rude cabdriver, a universal ideology (what else to aspire to?) Last night I saw the sect of flagellants in the garden below: they were stamping their feet in the snow and warming their hands by a bonfire, looking more human than I'd seen anyone look in a while. Maybe there's nothing wrong with identifying yourself in terms of your needs. If you hide who you are then *that's* your identity. I can see it in your eyes.

MAYBE YOU CAN DEFINE LOVE IN TERMS OF WHAT IT ISN'T

& get back to me—
I have a call on the
other line.

*

The rays of light contain you like
something you might see that exists, but
who can remember the sins I committed
as a kid—did I call them that
innately or was it just a trick to
make me think more about what *I* wanted,
was that the sin? Describe a paradigm
in which nothing ever repeats itself,
a love you might consider an achievement
or an act of will. You didn't let it die
but stayed true to your own idea of
constancy no matter what anyone else thought
about what you did. Sometimes my actions
belie what I feel, isn't that human?
It's not a sin to step outside yourself
& find something pleasurable about the
light & air, but a sin to deny yourself
pleasure, any shape or form, as it comes
your way. The end
of the story congeals before it begins.
Textures of paint (if the walls could speak etc.)
ruminate on some silence, something said.

*

I'm locked in the bathroom at the party at Bill Berkson's mother's house. Keep turning knob but the door is stuck. Finally, I begin banging on the door and calling out for help, until a woman I'd been introduced to earlier comes to my rescue. "I thought it was a ghost," she says. We lean back against the sink, with its gold faucets, and kiss.

*

The precedent to what I felt
doesn't exist in history (cf Michelet)
but a kiss is more ignoble than the tomes
of antiquity, a kiss is not entered
into haphazardly but with eyes wide open

*

a helicopter just flew over
the lake like a brushstroke
& the same sun I saw yesterday
disappeared behind a tree,
the sun's light seems less
intense this year, don't you think?
the wind just blew the pink
inner tube beneath the dock,
one remains justly yours, now & forever
but the kiss is like statuary, blown
to pieces by the storm

*

"I've lost the will to be prodigious"
one might say, or just "I've
lost it"

*

The unattainable. Falling in love with someone who's already "attached." A woman you see one day on the beach. Aspiring to the unattainable in poetry (& in love too).

*

in the afterglow of something
passing like a bird through the
treetops there's the sound
of hammering I heard yesterday &
the days vanish & with them this
thin wafer of desire pressed
under the tongue in all its
purity dissolves in its entirety
leaving a bad taste, a grown-up taste,
a refinement of every taste
I've ever known, something "mature" as
some people might say though maturity's
just a form of reticence in its way,
a state of decay

*

I took LSD for the first time at Liam O'Gallagher's loft in San Francisco. After a few hours I decided I wanted to be alone, hopped the cable car up California Street to my apartment on Nob Hill. Back home, I "thought" I'd come down & figured I should probably eat something—it had been awhile. I made myself a steak & some frozen vegetables & sat down at the small table looking out at the garden. When I realized I couldn't lift my knife & fork in the proper manner it occurred to me that the drug had changed me in a permanent way, that I'd never be the same person again. Not only wouldn't I ever eat again, but I wouldn't write poetry either.

*

There must be incentives
other than acquisitiveness & fear
that make us want to do one thing
more than another

*

"We met by the Xerox machine," David, a bond trader, relates. "She'd just been hired, & I was enthralled. I can't put my finger on anything she said or did, but I was certain, *certain*, that she felt the way I did. We were chatting about God knows what, nobody else was around, & I said to myself, 'I'm going to do it this time, I'm going to grab her right here, run my hands down her, kiss her till our teeth turn to powder.' And then I thought, 'Holy God, what if I'm wrong? What if she starts screaming?' So I just stood there on the edge like that, chatting pleasantly, like a pitiful helpless giant."

*

we're kidding ourselves if we think
we can accomplish everything,
in the time that's allotted us
let's do all we can without putting
off till tomorrow & in general

prevaricating about everything the way
we did in the past when time
had that feeling of infinite longing
like looking into the eyes of a cat
or dog & realizing this animal isn't
looking at you but at something you can't
see that's beyond you (infinite space & air)

*

it might happen that you would
consider someone else's feelings, &
in that way learn something
you didn't already know

*

It's Washington's birthday. Beverly takes Marie to *Amadeus*, I take Max to Washington Square Park. Bernadette stays at home (to work on the dollhouse) with Sophia. Blue sky through the branches & the flag waving in the breeze.

*

"Does this mean that whatever exists does, in some sense, contain you?"

Is the whole of creation too small to hold God?

overlapping—"is the same part of you present in all things at once?"

"Who can recall the sins I committed as a baby?"

"grown-up games are known as 'business'"

"every soul who sins brings its own punishment upon itself"

*

should we state our needs
clearly or keep them secret
like the bird
we know
desires warmth & attention
but what if it learned the meaning
of words like "desire" & "want"
would we allow its
feelings to take precedent
over our own
or would we remark to ourselves   imagine
as we often do, about people
what it would be like
to be a bird   see
the world through
                        her eyes

*

To be alone with oneself
is beautiful, & that indigenous phrase

like all human contact ripening on the stem
& the voice inside still speaking for everyone.

Latching on to something & then holding back
as if frightened I'd gone too far, only it wasn't

my own soul I was looking into
but someone even more vulnerable, here

are her eyes in which I can see myself
& the vortex of a calm reflection

which isn't perfidious or the opposite
of whatever that might be, sublime?

*

one rails against the impertinence
of others, in the impersonal sense,
talking about poetry instead of sex

*

I take Sophia to see *Amadeus* (Saturday afternoon). On the way home we stop in Washington Square Park where I meet Bruce & his daughter. He's completely gray but still handsome. I know he's been in jail but we don't talk about it. Instead, we discuss apartments, real estate, different neighborhoods—how they're changing & where we might want to live. I tell him that my landlord offered me $20,000 to move. He tells me I should take the money & buy a building & rent it out. "You have to become a bit of a capitalist, Lewis."

*

Is love these two people
locked in a haphazard embrace? Or
is some more feasible entity
created that insists that something beautiful
must occur, pertaining to bliss,

& the desire to give—is that what it
means?

*

Says Toni, a senior vice president with a major cosmetics firm, whose affair with a colleague almost destroyed her career: "There was a time when women just didn't do any buying. The men traveled in packs, and their wives had the normal fear of one-night stands. Then, when a lot of women were promoted to that level, the wives would say, "You're not going on a trip with *her.* What do you mean, you're going for four days to Florida with *so-and-so!*" The men would say, "Don't be silly, it's business, I'm a *professional*, this is my job!" Well, that's nonsense. They may *set out* on business, but the temptations are enormous. You don't have to worry any more about how you're going to stay out for the evening and explain it to the spouse. I mean, you're totally free! You're in a motel, you're having drinks, and this young handsome guy whom you've just been talking to is in the room next to yours, and what the hell, you're in Kookamonga!"

*

it's your own opinion
I want to hear
not what others think
to convince you because
they talk louder, act
more aggressive
don't go home & worry
it's your passive self
that relinquished hold
on your ideals
in the face of a tirade

at the edge of the balustrade
hiding under an umbrella
like a subsidiary organization
whose heart is here
is present
in name only

*

Mohammed tells me he works at a bakery from 7 to 5, then goes to classes every night. He's trying to save money to bring his family here from Nigeria. He apologizes for sometimes falling asleep during my class.

*

Only the simple things matter now: making breakfast for the kids, taking them to school, reading them books & playing scrabble & bingo.

*

From now on nothing's going to seem real except the simple things like washing dishes & cooking dinner.

*

August 27, 1984

Dear Lewis,

I'm so happy that you wrote Your letter touched a deep place in me because it was so open and honest—I hope I can respond as openly.

I'm lying on my bed in my rambling, messy room—I haven't been feeling well for the last three days so I haven't been cleaning up very much.

It seems the only time I have time to write to my friends is when I'm sick, otherwise my life is so active and busy that I only slow down long enough to sleep.

I'm currently 'single' again. I've been in this relationship with Jim Durrell on & off for the last 2 years. I love him dearly, but he's a classic manic-depressive—5 months on top of the world followed by 6 months of deep depression & withdrawal. The withdrawal becomes so complete that he actually disappears, goes off on Monday morning supposedly to work (construction & carpentry) and isn't seen or heard from by anyone for long months.

This has happened twice in the course of these 2 years—and five or six times in his adult life. I might sound glib about it but it's actually pretty devastating for me. Last time it happened November 9 (your birthday) of 1982, he wasn't seen or heard from until April '83. During that time I felt a little bit insane, like there was a big piece of my mental jigsaw that was missing. This time (he disappeared again April 23rd—my 21st wedding anniversary with Denny) and I'm not expecting to hear from him till October (his birthday). I don't feel crazy, like last time, but I feel more heartbroken, and more hopeless about making another attempt at living with him.

Anyway, I dreamed last night that he came back and we fought immediately because during the year that we were together, April '83—April '84, I had asked him to promise that if he ever disappeared again he would leave me a note—he did promise but didn't leave a note—and that's what we fought about in the dream. Later in the dream (and this is the part that ties in with your letter) he told me that he wanted to come back & live with me, but only if I loved him absolutely and completely, that feeling that he didn't have 100% of my love is what drove him away as much as, if not more than his own cyclical mood swing, he said in the dream.

I woke up then and wondered if I would or had ever loved a man as completely as he wanted to be and we all desire to be loved. Which leads me to my present thoughts about exclusivity.

For the past 2 months (for the first 2 months after he was gone I was celibate and miserable), I've been experimenting with being purposely non-exclusive in my relationships with men. That is: having a lot of men friends and interacting with them however I feel and not settling into one relationship. Its been pretty hectic, but it has some great advantages. Mostly just a great feeling of personal autonomy and having my self in the center of my life rather than my relationship with Jim or Greg or Franklin or Tony or Vince or Layne (the six men I've been in primary, exclusive, monogamous relationships with in the past 16 years) as the center of my life. The other great advantage is that I'm not put in the position of wanting or trying to find one person that answers all my needs and complements me in all my facets. Jim's request in the dream that I love him to the exclusion of everyone else is impossible—I can be sexually monogamous (altho I'm not sure it's the way I prefer to be) but I can't be completely emotionally, intellectually, aesthetically or hedonistically monogamous.

And I think that inability on my part and on their parts has been the ultimate cause for all the break-ups, heartbreaks and misery that has followed the happy times in all six of those relationships. Why does it need to be this way?

I think we need to change, radically change, our expectations and ideals about what male/female relationships are and can be.

I think it's damn hard to live with one other person for 10 years without going stir crazy for other interaction—I think the only reason most people stick it out that long is because of children or finances or both.

But our generation is on the cutting edge of an evolutionary change and sometimes it seems more like the lunatic fringe than the cutting edge. It gets very crazy!

(Later)

I really enjoyed *Agnes & Sally.* As always, your amazing talent for portraying what goes on inside the most intimate confines of the human mind carried me from beginning to end.

In thinking about it afterwards I was trying to understand why I feel more fortunate than any of the 4 characters in the book, and I decided that the most obvious reason is that relationships are not the only passion in my life. A lot of time and energy and joy go into my dancing and singing. And I think it's true that one's art is a more durable and dependable soul alliance than most love affairs tend to be. Ours is an exception, I hope.

Well, sweetheart, I've written about all I can write for this night.

Let's try to keep this correspondence flowing.

I love you

Allegra

I enclose a photo of my beautiful daughter, who is currently dancing in my troupe. Send me a picture of yours. I've never seen Max.

Next day

I didn't sleep last night. Dark night of self doubt. Fearing "forty."

So much of my professional life and social life has been dependent on being sexy and beautiful and so much of being sexy and beautiful in this culture is dependent on being young.

And I wonder if I'm not being foolish and impractical in continuing to pursue a performing career—if I wouldn't be wiser to change my course and steer more toward teaching.

But I don't want to. I still have so much juice for performing.

I still harbor a lot of fantasies about group marriage—It somehow has always been my ideal. I remember wanting it with you and Jeremy—then with you and Denny—then with Denny & Jean & Vince—then with Michael, Debra, Sterling, Morae & Frederico—then with Solomon & Delys (all these incredible people who you don't know). Anyway, it never worked out for me. But I still haven't given up hope.

Lewis, it's time for me to stop. I have to go pick up my Dad (who's now well up in his 80s and very forgetful and much sweeter) and take him for his afternoon outing.

Watching the whole life process through the many generations of my family (my brother Jamie has 2 little girls) is quite amazing.

Hugs & Kisses to You & Yours

Allegra

*

I see some comprehension in life's sorrows, but
I turn away from the dark
for awhile I forgot my work—I had other things to do
jobs to earn money to eat & pay rent
I wandered through the world with dignity, saying
    hello—
& then taking your hand—or goodbye, & grasping your
    shoulder
in a friendly way
all day the rain tossed my boat against the shore
but ecstacy was a mirror

with a narrow frame
I could pass through like a door
arrive at some new place
(neither heavyset nor thin)
Sometimes I'd kiss someone I didn't know
just to show that affection was still possible
& just to see the look of surprise pass over her face
as if to say: Really! I didn't know you cared—

ENTERING NIGHT

There are fences around churches to keep the agony from
steeping

I wash the dishes by starlight, it's all I can do for today

You get the impression people are laughing at him behind his
back & that he doesn't care

Someday I'll come back to this street & say: I used to live here

The American woman in the Japanese restaurant opened her
blouse & massaged her breast as she talked to her
boyfriend who slouched in his chair

Won't order any new food in restaurant for fear I won't like it—
order only what I like, another ruined evening

They tell you it can't last because they don't want you to be
happy, people are like that I'm afraid

Don't think I'm being withdrawn if I seek refuge in my private
world

I used to play "Für Elise" but then I told my piano teacher
that I wanted to play "popular" music so he brought
me the score for "The King & I" & I quit taking lessons

All we could do when we got to the park was sit on the grass, eat
sandwiches, play ball

& so much to say, how long can I linger over this letter, among
the boxes of tea & sweeteners, don't take everything
for yourself

Before putting on mascara comb through & separate eyelashes
with an old toothbrush

You could hope for an act of generosity that wasn't someone's
idea of a deal, an exchange over a counter for some
commodity like the elixir of life

I know better than to think I'd debase my own feelings by letting
them stagnate like weeds at the bottom of a lake without
first tearing them up from the roots with my bare hands
& laying them down in a neat pile on the shore

I stand in the waves at Far Rockaway & in the little breakers
at Jones Beach & haunt the Russian restaurants &
tearooms beneath the el in Brighten & swear to myself
but I'm only a virgin in the shade of a tree on a blanket
with my parents

Tactics of evasion give rise to purity of experience

In many cases the petting is limited to simple kisses & caresses

I failed as a child & later with my lover I reached out for

We exist reciprocally in relation to ourselves & to one another,
but if you go too far away you might cry out "Mother,
I'm lost" & return to where you began, start again
with a new person

You might think this book contains everything I know, but
when you come to the end you say: he's never been
in love

To have the bodies of one's closest relations eaten by someone
else is not as good as eating them oneself

It's the light around the edges of the city not the innermost
self which speaks of trial & error in the judicial sense
where people are sent up the creek for so many years we
can no longer recognize them when we see them on the
street, alive & free

Sometimes he loses the thread of a thought & begins to mumble
to himself regardless of whether he's talking to someone
or he's alone, but we don't interrupt him: maybe he's
talking about us?

He deports himself as if he had tenure, but he can be fired
at a moment's notice

Guy in sauna says, "Give me a cigarette & a drink. What's all
this health shit anyway?"

Mummified deity come unbound: a struggle with loss is your
next obsession

Love isn't a person or a thing or an abstract noun meaning
itself or its derivatives nor is it a person replacing
an object which you might desire to sleep with, nor is
it inanimate, this person, nor can it speak, this
thing, nor can it return love, this harbinger, nor
stand on a pedestal, this star

& if we had but time to waste, to get wasted, I'd tell you
the story: I'd call you long distance

We can hum along with the song until the promise of pleasure
relates to a pronoun which in turn takes the form of a
person who isn't here

What you say about hell may be a fiction, but she still isn't
here

Each step of the day is a dwelling place for memories that
underline—some might say "amplify"—your present state,
by enfolding it in rigorous ambivalence of who you've
become, leaving no stone unturned to the light of day,
no moment sacred, while establishing a link of certainty
to the transience of the hours of solitude where thinking
"goes on" invisibly as an experience of what remains, the
imminent floundering about of everything, the fin of
a fish in the ship's wake

You can say of omnipotence a psychiatrist's sanity was
well-earned

My great grandfather spent most of his time in a synagogue on
Pike Street

If poetry arises from some hiding place then I want to sit down
& talk with that moral eunuch who envisioned the poem as
a medium between the heart & the brain

An acre of refinement that glows around the border like the
winning number in a drawing: there are no matching
socks

I need your attention to appease my anger

People wet their beds when they sleep in a new place for
the first time

Ideas attached to words look frail in comparison as if someone
were suffering from the catarrh that was going around

I fastened on a vocation before I knew who I was (my
identity is a function of my relations with others, not
what I do)

She rings the downstairs buzzer—I let her in

Moths blew in through the holes in the screen & a sick child
stirred in her sleep, this was pleasure

On Xmas Eve I hitched over Mt. Tam on the back of a
motorcycle

In his lexicon, the word "bourgeoisie" is an object of fear

Leaning your chin on your hand can cause acne—if your hand
is dirty

My father went into the hallway & began calling for the police
to save him from my mother whom he didn't recognize
& whom he thought wanted to murder him & steal his
money

Ask someone for advice & he says "all she needs is affection"

She was so surprised to meet him she didn't notice he wasn't
wearing his pants

It‘s time I look out the window, you pass this way, you say
you came a long way for nothing: sticker affixed to
appliance

He limits his experience to what he reads, but content intrudes:
the radio, heat coming up through the pipes, the words
of a song

I can’t read the blackboard but I’m too vain to wear glasses

The winds of the gods blow their words in my face

I want to go to a restaurant where the waiters call me "comrade"

There’s no risk if you know the results of what you do, no inner
growth in which recourse to action leads to attrition, no
flower so insular it can’t command its own fee

You can open the tomb in my presence & find the eraser

I guess they better recruit some new players to replace the old
ones who can barely get up the court on defense & tend
to stand around & watch the trajectory of the ball
in its arc as it leaves the hands of the opposing players

"Look," you said, at the seagull on the ledge, but when I turned
it had flown away

You look like someone I used to know, expressing dismay at my
pregnancy, maybe the weather

NO VICTIMS

At the end of the
vagina there's another
penis waiting for me,
but when I meet it
what will I do or say?

Sometimes the sky is
blue, sometimes it's white
or gray, filled with
clouds. She spends a
lot of time putting on

eye makeup and perfume.
An unknown man sits between
me and my wife; we're at
a banquet, someone says,
it might be my bar mitzvah.

Once I put on my father's
trousers and the waist went
up over my head—as if
my head were in my father's
stomach or heart.

Till death do us part, these
leaves wither and break off
from the branches, drift insidiously
to the floor of the garden.
Last year's love poems

look like they were written
by someone else, but it's still
the same person staring at me
in the pane of glass
as I walk by the bodega

on my way home from school.
The front is confused with
the back. My penis isn't where
I left it when I went to bed.
Which way is in?

ATHENS '69

My memories of being in Athens
are hazy, & filled
with a pain I don't
want to admit. I was
only there 3 days before I flew
to London. The people
on the streets of Athens
stared disapprovingly at my long
hair. I never got to visit the
islands: reservations on the boats
were booked weeks in advance,
though I might have gone if I'd been
more patient. I didn't want to wait: if
I stayed in one place too long I'd think
too much about why I was there.
They say the trip is more important
than the destination, & I think
that's true. It didn't matter
where I was. I'd boarded a plane:
it could have landed anywhere.
In the airport, they checked
my baggage for weapons.
On the bus from the airport
people were talking about politics.
The landscape was flat, like a desert, with
despotic shrubs (in my hotel, at night,
I thought I heard a coyote's bark).
I bought cigarettes in a kiosk in Constitution Square
& read the newspapers & drank coke in a cafe.
I never had coffee with the woman across the courtyard.

The day after I left, the Olympic Airways office
where I bought my ticket was bombed,
& I was too: in a flat in London, on mescaline,
I filed my thoughts of Athens
behind a trapdoor in the back
of my head. When someone
asks me what being there was like I tell
them about the men who would literally spit
at my feet as I walked by.

Who knows what happens.

MISTAKEN IDENTITY

There's a little fear piercing
the air at the boundary of the self

it's the same self I saw under the awning
back in '63

Yesterday we saw the mushroom with
the orange flecks that grew up
out of the earth after last week's big
rain

It seems like anyone could shoot an arrow
& pierce my heart

Of love, bursting into flame, I inhale
the sweet smoke, hidden under the pale
refrain of all the old leaves

& now some leaves are falling
around the steps of the porch

& the wizened fish under the dock
are suffering
in our absence

MIRROR'S EDGE

Someone pushes us aside to get a better
view. This is known as entrapment, the threat
of what happens if you don't take precautions.
A lie stuck in the throat, like compost festering
in an abandoned garden. If you sleep all day,
without making excuses, you can still cram
an hour with words and enter the world
victorious on a storm of hailstones. You can
picture yourself on the upper deck of
a bus in London or in the world's oldest
cemetery, stalking the graves, or on
an island in Greece, twisting the straps
of your sandals over your bare legs and ankles.
The soul is no longer confined to the boundaries
of the body, but reveals itself in every
gesture. A child lifts her mitten from
the snow and brushes it off with her naked
fingers. Hold back what you want to say for fear
you said it already: I think we spent a
night together back in '69, don't you know?
This photograph is the only proof I own that we
were ever part of the same landscape, a thread
hooked in the needle's eye stitching
our lives together, calcified and cold.

ELEGY

The leaves have a sense of
where they fall when they
return to earth

but as they dangle in the wind
like corpses swaying
from a branch

they replace the pure
space of their being
with an act of attention

which passes like
a lullaby through
the eye of a storm.

THWARTED SUITOR

One can be civil in the matter
of attending to the awkwardness that makes
disappointment in love a thing of beauty,
and love is the way of attending to this,
like the personal devotion to the image
of a face or thing. As I read her
thoughts the neck of the bottle turned
into a snake and the lamp I was reading
her thoughts by cast a shadow
on the sleeves of her shirt. What
might be the issues of the day you attend
to? One thinks to start a filling
station with a master plan
in which all oil and gas is pumped
directly onto the highway. One seeks
to marry an idea with a feeling. One
seeks pleasure from another in bed,
or elsewhere, one processes one's
sense of pleasure, one feels serene.
Passion is a way of diverting
your attention from everything else
you ever wanted to do or know. Pencil
in whatever you thought in the margin
as it occurs but don't let it attack
your sense of attention to something
that might not be worth remembering.
Remember it now as being more than an attitude
to something interminable or unrelenting
for in your attention to that you became
the person you didn't know

could change over night and still glow
like a fire, untended.

A MAN ESCAPED

Words escape through gaps:
meaning converts them into conduits.
Stained leaves. Dyed parchment
on which nothing is crossed out.
The words begin to swagger through the
whiteness of a last refrain,
then draw back, seductive, as if no
longer responsible, compromising
themselves like a series of defective vehicles
that have to be shipped back to the factory
from the dealership window.
Invective in a starling's mouth,
refracting pleasure down to the last decibel.

TO THE HOUSEHOLD GODDESS

Am I all on the
surface or is part of me
inside or am I mostly
inside with only
a few parts surface?

What leaves a lasting
impression is finality, finally
what remains when you're
gone, not dying. That much
love can't go

around to everyone:
must make a funnel
to the appropriate
source of feeling
or appropriate a feeling

before it rusts. Thunder
at midnight is nothing to own
in the world outside your window
a stone is visible in the dust like
a message from the sun on my desk.

AVENUE OF ESCAPE

She pretends that she's kissing him but their lips never meet

The cop stopped us outside Alberqueque & we dropped our dope
on the side of the road

I had a way of hinting at what I was feeling without coming out
& saying it

My sister teaches me to dance the lindy

Many separations end in reconciliation, although many of
these reconciliations will later give way to new
separations

The guy who replaced him had no prior experience but was
willing to work for less than minimum wage

I had an alibi for where I was on the night of August 28, 1985
but the police still subpoenaed me to give testimony at
a closed hearing

We hire someone else, a third party, to do our dirty work

When I was thirteen I got up on a stage in a house of God
(so-called) & sang a song whose meaning the meaning of
which was in the inflections of the words

A 2-ton trailer truck overturned on the Belt Parkway causing
a tie-up on the Gowanus Expressway

I sing the emphasis of sound to convey meaning to somebody

I go to the store to buy some scallions

The obsession with undoing the processes of the past, the past
actions & thoughts, until they're null & void

Once I was a hysteric, now I'm an obsessive-compulsive

Tchaikovsky's 2nd Piano Concerto on the radio: I'm too lazy
to turn the dial

I shared a hotelroom in Barcelona with a guy I met on the train
who washed his underwear in the sink while I slept

She was wearing flat shoes, a white turtleneck, & over the
knee socks

They found out the results of the test: positive, positive,
positive

It might be sad to note that there are instances when words
correspond with reality, like the word "reality" when you
speak it, & the clouds pass in front of the sun

We wanted to go to the movies but I couldn't find a parking
space so we rented a movie at the video store & went
home & watched it

All the roaches in the drawer are pregnant

The ancient cutting off the branch of the forget-me-not
grows to fruition

You can sleep over on the couch if you don't want to go home
alone

The girl said she saw the murder from the window of her
apartment, but no one believed her because of her history
of drug abuse

Nothing I do can make her happy

The restaurant turned me away because I wasn't wearing a jacket
& tie

It wasn't as if I could tell what she was thinking, or wanted
to, but it was like the sun had vanished behind a cloud,
all the light faded from her eyes, & I didn't have to ask
"What are you thinking?" or "What's wrong?", I could
tell what was on her mind by the way she crossed her
legs & tilted her head

The people who spoke out against his policy were confined to
their cells

Three to five with time off for good behavior, twenty-five
to life with no possibility of parole

Out the window, in a moving vehicle, thinking & reading

I may be old, but I'm still desirable

She told me she was pregnant, that I was the father, but that
she was marrying someone else

The distance between stars can be measured in feet & inches

The prison warden's wife runs off with an ex-con

He smiled, & every tooth seemed to have a new meaning

There's no future in becoming something if you can't accept who
you are in the present & realize that the person you're
in the process of becoming is a close relation to the
person you are now

The therapist adjusts her skirt over her knees

She was 8, he was 14, they met in the basement, she touched
his penis

It doesn't take a genius to realize that combining strong
analgesics with liquor in great quantities can bring
hidden personality traits to the surface

He sat in a corner waiting for someone to notice him

The elevator to the lobby was filled with young doctors

I strain my neck staring at the ceiling of the Vatican

You can say I felt helpless, dependent, like a young child
who just bit his tongue, but when someone paged for a
doctor on the intercom I snapped to attention

No one suffering from minor trauma, no one climbing the walls

The Latin teacher accuses me of cheating on the final exam

I could tell what she was thinking by the way she looked at me
as if I wasn't there

It wasn't my nature to depend on my family for salvation but
if I ever became desperate I would wire them for some
money

You can pay me back, without interest, a little at a time

The whole class was punished because one student was cheating

The guy at the next table raises his beer bottle in my direction:
"Hey Bro!"

"I don't think I want to win anything, I want to die unadorned"

The fighter in orange trunks shrugs his robe onto the carpet

It's no longer appropriate to mention our names in the same
breath

An announcement for a tag sale tacked to the trunk of a tree

I remove her denim skirt, her basketball sneakers, her golf cap

Hold back real feelings so they exist in new form complicated by
not 'exposing' them to reaction of someone who
hates you

The matinee was no longer during the day, but after hours, when
even the quietest street turned its back on tranquility

It's not just because we're human that we want to experience
everything

Once they sat in a theater, alone in their heads

I say things out of nowhere to draw attention to myself,
    otherwise I am nowhere

You can let love die without anyone knowing it

There's a half-hour delay at the Lincoln & Holland Tunnels

The man at the entrance to the alley glanced over his shoulder
    as he buttoned his pants

ENMESHMENT

I listened to the voices that shattered
my heart, strange prerequisite, followed
by silence (I was an unrequited lover
again), my being contained an ampersand
dividing me from others & me from myself,
& the others (like plants desirous of light
& water) reflected through other eyes the casualness
of what I said, I could be aggressive, I could
be a "type" of person, I could even live a lie,
one imagines a bowl of light & a volatile bottle
which we could use to dynamite the walls of a public
building, I could harbor resentment till it flew
over my head like a dagger & passed through the heart
of an innocent bystander, one might look dumbstruck
in comparison to others for whom knowledge was a cherished
companion, my dependencies demand compensation
(an eye that opens like a shutter), I had what
you might call a "breakthru" but which for me
was "normal love," I wore the straight-jacket
of love's decline like the door of a locked room
with two people cowering behind it, I read how
achievement had nothing to do with the possession
of property, I had lunch with Peggy
but I couldn't eat (when it came
time to order all I could say was "I'll take
the same"), there was no distinction or space but
there was room for improvement, I saw myself as a special
plant or flower, a wild bleeding heart or black-eyed
susan, but I forgot about immunity & the right
to remain silent, I thought of affection as a way

of expressing something to someone you loved
(in the simplest sense, like brushing the hair
out of a person's eyes), I grew accustomed
to cold spaces, unmade beds, dishes in sink
the laundry piled up on the bathroom floor, a couch
with no legs, I saw anger as a way of slipping
down a well with no sides, I limited myself
to what was most fortuitous, a rock or shell
washed up on the shore, I climbed tenement steps
to find an island with a broad vista
& discovered a window with a transparent curtain & a bamboo
    shade
I denied love's passage into memory, & all the digressions
blue earrings, a furrowed brow, two shadows on the page.

GRACE NOTES

But losing out, losing
one hair out of
the darkness, losing
the thread of
conversation, simply

losing one's way &
winding up
in a forest
with others like you—
has nothing to do

with loss of love,
identity loss & speech loss,
the loss of one's lover,
what it felt like
to be young. It has

little to do with
seeing the world through
a monocle, or rekindling
your feelings so
that you can live

among the trolls.
The desiccated glass
feeds on the reflection
of an open door, a voice
in the other room,

footsteps, the turn of a key.
We listen at the confessional
for the progress of materialism
to set an example, but we won't
lift a cudgel to the door

of the sanctuary. In time,
pleasure finds an empty
carriage for our posthumous
songs. Can a bird petition mythology
for a place in the pantheon?

Will we ever stop doting?

EVIDENCE

I walk to 14th Street to make
a mailbox key for my wife. I
buy a stamp and mail a letter.
"Let's live together again," it
says, in so many words. I watch
the letter slip from my hand
into the blue and red mailbox
outside the postoffice. Three
XXX rated movies are playing in
a nearby theater. Some men are playing
dominos outside a bodega
on Avenue A. Inside the bodega,
a ballgame, and cool shadows.

THE POSSESSED

"When I was eight my piano teacher, Mr.
Ussum, used to touch my knees & breasts
during our lessons. He would press my forehead
with his hairy fingers. My friend, Irene,
who also took lessons from Mr. Ussum, told me
that the same thing happened to her.
Neither of us made any attempt to stop him
when he touched us; & neither of us told
our parents."

Maybe it's our duty to spend our old age together.
Stay in touch. Things come around.
There's so much time in between then & now, but
the time between now & later seems to be growing
shorter. It's not our last chance, but almost,
though I wouldn't say we're wasting time
& I don't lose any sleep over it though
some nights, up at 4 or 5 AM, I lie
awake & stare at the ceiling a few inches
from my face & think of the night you got drunk
in the bathtub, fully-dressed, at a party
& cut your hand, purposely, on a broken bottle.
You were 15, & I loved your craziness.
It made me feel needed, like maybe
you'd die if I wasn't around.

ACTUAL SIZE

A neon sign is blinking
on & off & it's raining
& the cars are going by,
the kids are watching TV &

eating donuts, the phone's
ringing & I'm looking
out the window
from the edge of the bed.

*

I help a stranger carry a package up
the stairs. It's the webbing
in my hand that hurts in the afterglow.
It's the attachment of my body
to people & things that causes anxiety
in the rush of memory. You can't let go
without breaking something.
The earth is no more dense than water
& things fall through it & disappear.
Into this mesh of days you made an entrance
that consisted of fragments of all the flowers
& their names, you entered without
bowing to anyone but yourself, without casting
an aside to your reflection in the full-
length mirror. For a moment, I thought of you
as out of reach, insinuating vague polarities
without replenishing the chains. Our history
had not yet started, so to speak.

You took your seat in a class, among others.
When I asked you your name I forced you
to say it again. "Can everyone
hear in the back?" I shouted.
At night, I drafted a kiss but it
emerged as a forgery on skin that was
already coated with petals. But once
the fog lifted I regaled in the regrets
of a new equilibrium for which there were
no witnesses. And when I finished reading
there was no applause, only a cry
from the balcony, as in a cheap
restaurant, for "seconds." The man
behind the counter taught
Latin in his homeland, but
circumstances had reduced him
to a purveyor of cold cash. The heart
hardens at the thought of promises
unkept & solutions with pickets
to hoist over stones. One imagines
oneself in the center of a strange city,
on a planet preoccupied with dirt
& amusement, the transfiguration of
sound particles (as in a liturgy) into
sanctified space. "If the earth fits,
if the shoe fits..." but memory is effortless.
Here's a sponge to wipe off the crumbs
of denial, an emerald occasion.

OPEN ALL NIGHT

I wanted to believe as if there was no precedent
The woman who sits near the hydrant with her kids

One could put value on anything that flows through
    something, like plasma
A different type, everyone you see on the street

I was envious of them for their communion
How they could all suffer together, in unison, day after day

What you see is one person, singly, no longer confused
While other thoughts mingle, less abstruse, passing
    through you

She sewed her own dress for the dance to "stand out"
She said, from the others, who shopped at the outlet

There was a loop in the story
On which I could hang my hat

Description appears with obligatory monotony
Words attributed to another were spoken aloud

There's always a new crisis to unsettle
The process of meaning

I ripped her dress without meaning to
As we collapse on the couch

Emotions that level meaning
Replace sense with laughter

Once I was alone, waiting for her
To cross the room & speak

As an author, I'm more like an infant
Than a psychotic

I dreamed about a tan raincoat with a belt
Which I hadn't worn in twenty years (when

I wore it the woman in the elevator
Said: "You stink")

The stores along Fordham Road were going out of business
I went to a night game at the Polo Grounds with my friend

We go to the dance together but I leave with another
I make the mistake of wanting what I can't have

Joy replaces meaning, like a new pendant
She was wearing black trousers, a fedora, chunky beads

Women selling *The Watchtower* had an inner glow
That lit up the station, but no one's listening

The search for continuity leads me down a blind alley
Where I end up writing what someone else wants

He said, "lighten up," as if the object of sanity was
    worth money
Put some weight on the words "estrange" and "forgotten"

When he told her he'd been in prison
She asked: "Where's your tattoo?"

He wants to marry me but first
I have to sleep with his closest friend

On his knees, when it was hottest
In August, & the ball game was over

Not jealousy so much as acceptance:
Myself & others

As far as I could go in the hallway in my robe
My sister closes the bathroom door to undress

As seahawks fly backwards during a storm
No one's concerned with what I've done & thought

The truth of life is that it ever happened
Some men in the street were begging for old clothes

By the fact that it can't go beyond itself
All these failures, speaking & writing

"I like your dress," I said, as I helped her on with her coat
"I'm pregnant," she said, as we met on the street corner,
"& it's your baby."

BLACK BREAD WITH RUSSIAN DRESSING

Cosmonaut, turn your antiquated gaze
to heaven, know no greater love
when the heart's awake

the gods originate in original sin
1 of a kind objects
and novelty items

made to order shirts with
centipedes stitched on the collars, hats
with brims to hide the eyes

like visors. Whenever I see her
I look the other way, she
crosses the street

when she sees me coming. Once
we were people who knew the special
way people feel when they meet

under complicated circumstances.
You might interpret the same event
differently. Water condenses

under room temperature, like poetry.
The caress of a hand still animated
by the thrill of discovery

without yet being blunted by desire
is only a memory.
Were we fixated forever

at that stage or did we change?
The highpoint of the visit was steak in an all-night diner,
a midwestern variety, she was leaving the next day.

Bite the delicate fingers
that feed you, and portray
it all in bas relief

on the side of a cup, alongside
the astronomical observations
so far ahead of their time

blueprints of buildings
with fake facades
and corbeled arches.

ELECTIVE SURGERY

You think you can begin as if it were ten years ago & you were
still that person

A woman turns her head to catch a glimpse of her former lover

I offer you the key to a city without words

The guy on trial for rape wears glasses to make him look studious

The policeman arrested the soldier for fondling a single parent

Sometimes I create an imaginary aisle in my mind: we're walking
down it, arm in arm, into the sunlight outside the church

The woman who approached my car & asked for a light wasn't
a prostitute

You can escape your responsibilities by going to the movies or
getting drunk

She picked him up hitch hiking & they lived together for three
years

The only person's feelings that I'm hurting are my own

Spaces that are only a dream of space, clouds that change shape
as they pass over the rooftops, flowers that speak in
flower language

Procreation isn't the only reason for fucking

He escapes his responsibilities by thinking about the past

It's possible to walk into a bar, depressed & alone, & leave
hours later with a new set of friends

She unzips her dress in front of an open window

Behind each window, behind every curtain, a person is dying
or sleeping

There are people dying, even as we speak, while others are
sleeping or in love

I can remember it all as if it happened yesterday: the kids
running down the hill to the dock, the woman on water
skis disappearing beneath the waves, the dead fish
floating on the surface of the lake

The fish aren't large enough to eat so they throw them back in

We go down to the dock to feed breadcrumbs to the fish

The words get lost in the shadow of the page

Let's fuck one last time before we're old & stupid

All he could see of her body was the neck & the ankles

I make the connection between the body of a woman & a
country, my mother

I live inside the body of a woman who isn't my mother

There's this new country across the ocean that resembles
my mother

Give me a ticket to the land of milk & honey

The I.R.S. writes me a letter saying I owe them $6,500.65

I was standing in front of the class with paintstains on my
shoes

I thought I'd discovered a new country but it was the same old
person, my mother

My brain is an airport with no departures, no goodbyes

You come up behind me & cover my eyes with your hands

He purges his emotions until one thing remains

He had lost so much weight I could encircle his upper arm
with my hand

One shrinks from the ineffable as if to ward off a blow

Some idea of perfection but no sense of value, the perfect
thought

Express & registered letters take longer than regular mail

A poem is more like a tree than a shoe

Tenderness was resurrected as a model of empathy

Our founding fathers in their undergarments on the pages of
Vogue

I was lead to believe that the job was mine for the asking but
when I showed up Monday morning they told me they
had hired someone else

An usher leads us down the aisle to our seats

All I know of the song "Mr. Blue" are the words "I'm Mr. Blue"

I know the words of "I've Got A Lovely Bunch of Coconuts," but
no one asks me to sing it

The little room has a purpose the way Puritanism has a purpose
but we don't want to go into it & talk about sex, we
don't want to pay someone to sit on a bed & talk about
sex

There's a little anger lurking in the corner of my heart

From here, it looks like a scar where the road turns on the way
to oblivion

I have a relationship with someone other than myself

My father looks up at us & says: you're not my family

Until yesterday, the word "orderly" wasn't part of my vocabulary

A person I felt close to fades out of my life

The cautious parent takes his child to the infirmary

I grew addicted to the feeling of being needed

He called the suicide hotline but received a busy signal

All this could happen when you were still a virgin

The phone rang & some guy asked to speak to my daughter

I want to tell you something, but you have to promise not
to repeat it

As we said goodbye I put my hand under her sweater under her
coat

The fragrance of a flower charged with meaning

I cut myself shaving, but it was only an accident (nothing
serious)

OVERTURE

We went to the hospital but no one died
It seemed like if we were careful we might come back alive
I had the keys to my parents' apartment in my pocket, just
in case
A young woman with a man who might have been her lover
Or her father buried her head in her hands
And told a stranger, not myself, that she was having an attack
An anxiety attack which is some form of dying
And the older man put his hand on her arm
And looked calm, a hand on the arm
Might help in an emergency, anything does
Anything's better than a baffled silence
Interrupted by an insipid remark about the weather
In small towns people talk about the weather and think about sex
I thought the woman with the older man who was having
an attack
Was someone I might marry, in another context
The people in the emergency room were watching a house burn
down on television
But I couldn't tell whether they were watching the 11 o'clock
news or *Baretta*
I've gained some weight recently, no one cares except you
Only one relative or friend is allowed at
The patient's bedside at the same time
When my first daughter was born
In Cooley Dickinson Hospital
On the outskirts of Northampton, Mass.
The head nurse ordered me out of the delivery room
While my wife was in the last throes of labor
Though I'd been with her non-stop for twenty-four hours

But I returned, insistent, saw the arrogance in my daughter's
eyes
Then careened into the night to my motel
Where I took a sleeping pill, and in the morning
Ate a huge breakfast in the Florence Diner
In Florence, Mass., before returning to the hospital
To see my new family
The leaves look petrified as they gather
On the fringe of the sky
There are bodies on stretchers waiting to be admitted to private
rooms
There are two patients to a room, or four, the Polish man
Who shares a room with my father
Suffers from asthma, my father
Leans on my arm as we walk down the hall
He tells me he's going to have an operation to improve his sex
life
My mother called to tell me he couldn't stand up
And when I arrived at their apartment
With my second daughter, who was born at home, delivered by a
midwife
On the night of winter's first snowstorm
The ambulance was already waiting out front
It was 90 degrees at 9 PM, no breeze, and the ambulance driver
Said: "It's going to be a McSorley's night," apropos of nothing.

BY THE FIRE

I turned the corner & there was
a goat. It had a bell around its neck
to get it where it wanted to go. Sometimes
there was a golden line that froze in the sky, like the
line that ran down the center of the road,
dividing the road in two as it disappeared
under the car. When I wanted to go somewhere
I stuck out my thumb. What are the customs
of this planet anyway? Isn't anyone home?
I forgot the manners & grace of calling in advance
to say "I'm coming over." I entered unannounced,
without knocking, as if no one cared. Everyone's home
was where one sat down & made oneself invisible, until someone
recognized you, saw you were there, nodded & said "hello."
I passed through town years ago & then I disappeared
but when I returned you were sitting in the same chair.
The house had a roof, four walls & some doors
& a lot of trinkets that someone had brought up
over the hill from the city. I ate an apple
on a rock at the edge of the shore. It could be
that if I got angry I might go to sleep anywhere
& that the next morning someone would find me, assure
me that nothing was wrong. I've never been able
to stay angry at anyone too long. I bought
the cheapest wine & drifted through life in a manner of speaking,
watched the words slip like peas off the end of
my knife. Some mornings I woke with a bad taste
in my mouth, as if I'd mistaken the edge of the plate
for some beans. It might be a good idea not to go
anywhere for awhile, stay put for once in your life

& watch the light pass through the tops of the trees.
I was crossing the field when you stopped & took off
your pants. I was standing on a reef looking down
on a roomful of props. It seems possible that
one can feel jaded from too much love, or from turning
yourself inside out till you become the other person
& she was the sky & the field you were walking through
lead to a tent or the basement of a deserted house.
But it was someone else's bedroom where the sun drifted in
through the curtains & I stepped over a puddle & listened to
the dogs bark just to get to where you were. Was I a fool
to leave you, lying in the sun, untended? In the storm,
when the electricity went out, we ate by the light of the hearth.
You never thought I could learn anything & when you spoke
I pretended not to listen but the next time I made it clear
that I'd thought it out for myself & that my manner
of knowledge was my own: the way I did things worked
out all right even if I didn't do them *right*, in the traditional
sense, as if for you there was only one right way
of doing anything, & that was all. You were frightened that my friends
were coming to displace you, so you left, but
before that I walked to your house every night.
I bought bread & wine, we ate by the fire.
It seemed like you had gone to bed before
me & then I was there, but that there were
no more tears or anger or recriminations & that our pasts
had dissolved at last like some huge stalagmite
on the wall of a cave. It was Plato's cave, & the
light at the entrance was like a sprig of juniper
around your eyes. I heard you coming but I didn't know
whether it was you or the horse in the pasture outside
the house. It wasn't your house: you were renting it
from someone else. I came along around 5 every night.

I climbed the hill, with groceries: did I call you
before I came? You were often in the kitchen making
dinner when I arrived. We drank some wine & ate
in front of the fire. I don't think
anyone visited us there, in our house. It
lasted awhile: me waiting, walking up the hill
with the food. I liked the way the trees looked & I was
in love with the past, with someone else, & you tried to steer
me closer to the present with your love for
me that was like all the fireflies & the leaves
of the eucalyptus trees that shadowed the road
as I walked through the door. Occasionally someone
I knew stopped their car & drove me halfway. I remember
the place where the road turned & I had to step over
some old logs. It was worth it to see the light in the window
& drink the wine. You were there in the kitchen, I wiped
the rain from my glasses, we embraced. Sometimes the
wires went down & we built a fire, we made dinner on the fire.
You taught me how to build a fire but thought I wasn't
listening. It was like reading the Odyssey by
candlelight, it was like travelling through the desert
to a wisp of smoke that was like an oasis of peacefulness not
a mirage of fear & sleep, not a deathmask but all the wishes
of childhood in the warmth of a blanket & a soft bed.
These feelings could extend from me to you & go on forever
as long as memory winds around the edge of the horizon
like a trail leading from town to town. I can be
myself, at last, & say we share this like a parcel
of land, divided in two, no fences: that's where we are.
I brought some wine & some bread & watched as you twisted
the corkscrew into the bottle & pulled the cork free &
poured the drinks. Was it raining outside? I can't remember,
but it's like a dream to forget the awning of trees

& the lights in the distance where you kneel by the fire
    with the kindling,
brown hair shining on the edge of a star.

MARRIED NAME

The miracle of technology
translates feelings into
sounds, but the flesh understands
whole sentences, & the organ
music plays on. It was no miracle:
her mantilla floated like a veil
over her shoulders. There was a well
with no water where we could
count the crevices in our skin.
Some people push forward
& trample innocent bystanders,
tourists who don't know better
stand like cattle in the rain.
I heard music from an old Wurlitzer
that seemed to be calling my
name. My hand between her legs
as we enter the shrine.

"Good luck" we translate, as
we cross the border, "good riddance."
Fake Indian jewelry echoes
down the ravine. All the usurers
on the level of hell I can't
remember which point their fingers
in our direction as they go under
for the last time. There's friction
in the air about who suffered most,
a drawer filled with carbons. We
were sitting in a Mexican restaurant
on the main street of Del Mar.

A rat in a maze, running backwards, but
no impressions of intimacy. I was
kneeling at the foot of the throne,
or so I lead you to believe. (Dark glasses,
bruises on thighs, broken ribs.)

Creatures of habit so decorous
in their enlightenment, the unanswerable
questions fill me like so much cheap food.
List price 80 pesos I'll give it to you
for a dollar: no, that's a dollar
off the price on the tag. The sins of
the fathers in the hands of the masseuse.
A "no vacancy" sign blinks at the foot
of the hill (a statue of a woman with her
hands chained behind her back). Devotion,
diversion, a list of temptations in love's
shadow. We walked down the aisle into the
sunlight outside the church. I start my life
over again, thinking: "It's still me, but
I'm different." It's not impossible to compare
yourself to a flower or a tree. The door
to the porch is open. I have a callous
on my thumb.

BLUE TURBAN

Words of desire swim in the throat
of the bird like motes of dust in the
parched air, like the small hairs
that send the blood rushing through
my heart. Can pain make me smart?
Or is it a double entendre to be both near
and distant from the object
of desire, the mirror image
of yourself? Nothing's necessary
on this winter night but to get
into bed and relax. It's early in the evening
and the kids are asleep. How happy you seem
lying in bed all evening,
in your blue robe, a blue towel
wrapped around your head, drinking wine and
reading books of poetry, while the rain
falls on the rooftops, the windows
and streets.

DIFFERENT TRAINS

1

I'm coming home
in the rain with
no excuses,
I'm late
it's late in
the day to
give lies
credence, to
believe one's
own lie
(but I was just
talking to
myself), to
strike a nerve
alive with
the desire to
speak the truth,
to unnerve meaning
through clenched
teeth & open
eyes

2

I was brought up with a distorted
view of heaven. Took it to bed with me
but couldn't sleep. It was like
going to the store when my mother
asked & returning with the change in
my sweaty palm. Should I drop the coins
into the jar on the table in the foyer?
Heart says "yes," body can't decide.
My mother says "Is that you?"
as I walk through the gate.

3

The wind came off the page & embraced
me. *And then the words of the author
embraced me as well.* The wind blew the
pages forward & back. I lost my place,
I forgot what I was reading. Usually,
when I stop reading, I fold down the
corner of the page to mark my place.
I removed my reading glasses & put on
the glasses I wear to see distances.
I placed the book on the ground at my
feet & watched the wind rifle the
pages. I balanced the open book against
the stump of a tree & watched the wind
blow through the pages until all the
words were erased. I fell asleep in my
chair with a book open on my knees.

4

Who put the words inside your mouth?
They weren't there when I saw
you last. Someone speaking in capital

letters, surface thoughts (an
endless diatribe of anger & regret).
I'll probably die regretting not doing

this, don't you think? It's no joke growing old
in a place where there's nothing
to do. But I like the climate

of doubt that melts into parallel
lines & the fantasy of loving
two people at the same time.

5

There's another way of seducing someone
into doing what you want. A heart
blasted into space without
precaution, in the next life
you'll focus all your energy on
one person (if it kills you). If
I spoke (spontaneously) from the heart
I knew I could get her attention. Also,
it's possible to seduce someone
without even trying. Everyone
wants to seduce her but me.
Isn't that interesting?

6

Don't raise me to the heights
& then discard, that's all I ask.
Don't buffet an obsession so flimsy,
my nightgown caught on a nail.
The soul isn't responsible
for what it says. The grammar
of monotony when I see her coming.

7

Laura was sitting in the living room
watching television trying not to listen
to the sounds Janice and Bill were making
in the bedroom. Janice had asked Laura
whether she minded if Bill came home with
her and Laura didn't have the heart to tell
her that Bill had called every night that
week when Janice was at work. "It's just a
matter of time," he told Laura, "before Janice
& I break up." Laura didn't particularly care
whether they broke up or not. She was dozing
off when Bill came into the living
room with a towel wrapped around his waist.
He knelt on the rug and lifted her skirt and
she spread her legs so that her ankles were resting
on his shoulders. "You can scream
all you want," he said. "She's asleep."

8

The letter arrives
like an arrow
crossing the margin
of destiny, but
no one has the nerve
to break the seal.

I have neither tenure
nor benefits. My mother
gives birth to a laurel
branch in a dream.
Mild-mannered, well-meaning,
temper & cool.

9

words reverberate like
recently sharpened pencils
to address the air
they float through

sequin desert mirage
embody a season
without end

Once I lived in a house
with a pantry where I kept
a 40-pound bag of potatoes
& some jam jars in case
I wanted to drink some jam

you can tell whether a poem's
any good by the type of paper
it's printed on

not *Remembrance of Things Past*
but a memory of wasted time

here, at the drawing board, gnawing
a bone

the taboo about a bone
eating human flesh also
a tattoo about a rose, the eye
of the gorgon, someone's mother

Sex, not work: but
you're fired, we've hired
a *new* lover

where I am you said you'd be:
it was my father's promise

Amor equals action: I think
I crossed this bridge before. A
firefly alights on the hem
of her dress.

an earring so weighted with pleasure
it touches my shoulder

a gift of speech

tokenism but I am present
in this form alone

10 *Phaedra*

His erudition is daunting, but all
he can do is spout indifference
to my own concerns, which only concern him
in as much as he's in front of me
(can I ask him to kneel?), & how to make
myself apparent, even nude I'm unvarnished,
so that suicide might be one way to trip the real
& find him wanting.

11

Every place is the same. You can't
travel far enough away from your self
to make it seem any different. Sometimes
I fly away but only half of me is there,
disengaged from the part of me that
remained on the ground. I'm here—but
I'm remembering what it felt like to be
in that place. It feels like floating,
like flying in a plane, like looking
down. The farther I go the more I feel
I've been somewhere else, but
it's useless to cry out when you're
lost in space, a dot filling a hole
that didn't exist before you came.
They reserve a place for you, & you fill it,
overjoyed at being accepted,
but it's only a vague sense of longing
that keeps the plane soaring above the ground.
A feeling of antipathy lingers in the air.
I get off the plane & no one's there.

12

Some of them were prettier
& some of them were sluts
but the prettiest of the bunch
didn't have to give it away
to the guys who were most popular
doing my friends one at a time
all you have to do is fuck someone
& in the morning they treat you like crap
there's evidence to the contrary
that it actually gives me pleasure
& I consented to everything you wanted
without holding back & I wanted
you because it made me feel like a person
one of the types who would go all the way
just to brag later that I'd done it
really done it & if my parents
come home late or not at all
you can show up after school
& we'll do it in the basement
it was always my fantasy
to be with two guys at once
even if they weren't
the most popular in my class
at least I know I'll never
have to be alone
like some girls I know
who won't put out

13

All my words add up to a single
thought, don't you know? But
sometimes not thinking in words I
lose sight of the meanings.

Here is a set of rules
to justify your existence: we
all follow the same rules but
we can't depend on the sacraments

as instruments of salvation
to become someone we already
know. The idea that you can
depend on someone to respond

to your feelings was absorbed
into the idea of loss
that had nothing to do
with this person. No one

can gratify your need to
be loved. It's rare to find
one other person to fulfill
all your needs. All you can do

is focus your attention on one
other person & hope for the best.
All you can do is bury your head
under the blankets & weep.

14 *for Sophia*

Climb up the side of
a statue for a view
of the city, don't fall

The houses that seemed to be
out of reach, the entrance
to the subway where you retie
your shoe in luxury

Even the view of the river
a dead man's rattle
strikes a chord
in your feverish heart

Or so I told you
as you were starting
out: stay calm
cross at the corners

in perfect visibility

15

A mirror at the bottom of the world,
reflecting our arms & faces. A newspaper
on the table, unread. The television
turned down low or unplugged. The door
closed between rooms. The cat scratching
at the door, wanting in. A prescription,
the name of a doctor, a vial of pills.

A photograph of myself & my children on
a lake in the country ten years ago. All
words, my voice, the beginning & end
of a sentence. A person listening to what
I say, a shock of disbelief on her face.
The body in bed: at rest or asleep. A cup
of tea cooling on the bedside table.

16

Remember the time you came into the room
in your yellow jumpsuit? It was the first time
I saw you explode with laughter & energy.
Later you'd fall asleep in class, legs apart,
like an old woman. I ignored the repercussions
of student-teacher relationships. "Let's
have dinner," I said, harmless, not wanting
to seduce you. An empty solipsism sets
the soul in motion. My heart was empty.
I was looking for someone to love.

17

Nothing dominates silence like words
A derelict subscription to a magazine of poetry
The pages hiss with phrases like "despite this"
        & "togetherness"
Which we memorize & recite
Till the tea kettle whistles

Even the man selling incense on the subway platform
Rubs the back of his neck, his ego tightens
Like a caress
At the crash of dominos

I thought of the correctness of an attitude
To pleasure that would take into account
The domino effect of words collapsing
Into one another

The lines of the page were like the rungs of a ladder
Leading to heaven, & I was the medium
Through which they flowed back to earth

18

I went to bed with Providence but we didn't
fuck. "I like to make love, not fuck," she said,
to which I responded: "I like to do both."
Sometimes we walked to the outskirts of the city
& took pictures of dumps, diners, abandoned
garages. My convictions are real but I'm easily
discouraged. For nourishment all I need is a ration
of servitude, the futile anxiety (stop) between
(stop) stupor & frenzy, a trunk steeped with
soiled bibs. All I knew of her past was what
she told me in her sleep. You could say this was
the *raison d'etre*, in the oldfashioned sense,
for being alive, to be one of those for whom
happiness comes as easy as breath, but I'd be
lying to myself if I thought we could last forever,
that one night, as we lay in bed with the blankets

on the floor, hair matted to the silk pillowcase,
the cops aren't going to arrive with their clubs
& accoutrements & cart us away in the back
of their tiny trucks.

19

The truth of loving is knowing
it might someday end but it doesn't
prevent you from saying "I'll
never love anyone again." In the
giving up of who you are to
someone else, in the forgetting
of oneself, in the feeling
that you might strangle a person
out of love, that sweat can intermingle
so freely, the vortex of anonymity in
a stranger's kiss, is this a sin? I woke
up (I was talking in my sleep) on the
kitchen floor, the notes of "Für
Elise" drifting through an open window.
I was getting around all right
by myself, or so I thought (I even
held some love in reserve for the other
in case she returned). If you want
to take a giant step forward you have to
say "please" or "May I?" less you go
back to the beginning & repeat
your mistakes. You don't want
to hear what it feels like to be
me (separate from you) & who
can blame you? This fragment was

only something of what was possible,
a clearing in the densest wood, but
it's pointless to think of what
might have been: if no one
gives anything there's nothing
to have to begin with. Sacrificing
everything, without holding
back, & then making it happen
again. The giving up of who
you are to another, the giving in.

20 *(Coda)*

I know that somewhere it's written
in bold type on yellow parchment
for everyone to read, but the signature
an X on a line changes intermittently
& with some humor, so that bathing
stepping up out of the bath where
everything descends, is part
of what I miss, what I'm blocking out.
The story, I miss you, every few inches
another window, & you're looking back
at me from the ledge, bird-like, alive
to what's most real, the cars
on the parkway, no longer alive
to what I can almost feel
is you, listening & breathing
in the other room. Sobs intermittent
keys on a chain, to adore you, no, to
be impervious to your adoration.
To dominate is not to adore in pain.

No thought as impervious as the
clouds are, a natural wonder,
no longer exempt from suffering, but free—
& the air yields.

ANYONE BUT YOU

I went to pick berries on the road to paradise

They call themselves Communists but all they want are
dishwashers & big cars

A light without shadow generates an emotion without reserve

Members of the staff leave the institution after an 8-hour shift,
but the inmates stay forever

He can ask someone for money without losing his self-respect

My mother didn't know what I wanted for my birthday, so she
gave me some money

I put my money on Awe Inspiring but it came in last

Border violations between genres were reported by the authorities

Type poems on stencils, run them off on the mimeo machine, call
up friends to help collate & staple, mail copies into
the world

I have some knowledge of her but maybe I'm thinking of
someone else

I think of what I'd say, what I could possibly say, if we ever
met

The place becomes the words you use to describe it but your feelings about the place have a life of their own

At parties we went to the bedroom where the guests stashed their coats, locked the door, swept the coats onto the floor, & took off our clothes

I changed my religion to please her parents, but they still hated me

New words are needed to heal the rift

We avoid each other in the bookstore, we pretend we don't see each other, I think you must feel guilty for not answering my last letter, you don't realize how much I love you, your last book was great

There's a beach all for yourself with a sign that reads "No Trespassing" tacked to a tree

How fortunate we are to be separate from the sea at last (mer = sea, mère = mother)

Mansions where executives once lived with their families will be split into apartments for the families of the workers

The cab driver orders me out of his vehicle: I owe him 17¢

I postpone pleasure so I can enjoy it more later, boredom of expectancy when no one comes

We go to her house & sit on the living room sofa while her parents sleep inside e.g. maybe tonight she'll let me put my hand inside her blouse

The desire for objectivity harbors the intrusion of jealousy

It seems like you might never stop loving her, & then you do

There's the movie theater where I saw *Rocco & His Brothers*
    (dubbed version), there's the schoolyard where I played
    "asses up"

In the fairy tale, a wedge of cheese falls from his beak into
    a puddle

We can't tell the players on the scorecards without sleeping
    with them

Last year at this time, or ten years ago, or twenty, a quarter
    century passes by as if it were a quarter hour, or a minute

When I was nine I hit a girl on the shoulder with a stone to
    get her attention

This house will never be empty of the torment of loving

We heard on the news that Deng Xiangping had died, but it was
    only a rumor

"No sweat" one might say as the solution to anything

I took a special speech course in college because of my lisp

Madonna's "Like A Prayer" on radio in schoolyard: it's the first
    day of summer

We smoke a last cigarette together before changing the sheets

I can spend in 5 hours what it takes me 3 days to earn

The used car salesman told me that he had a Buick with 130,000 miles on it for $1,600 that ran like a dream

I was in bed with her, in a dream, and her husband came in & said: I'm going to shoot you

I return home even though I know she's in bed with someone else

I opened the door with my key but she had put the chain on before she went to bed

Five Cubans calling for the ouster of Castro handcuffed themselves to a railing inside the crown of The Statue of Liberty

You return home on a crowded subway late at night full of resentment

Employers not only refuse to take on employees passed the age of 35 but hesitate to put their confidence in someone who has never been "permanently employed"

You light a thin cigarette & then put it out after taking one puff

You go out for a container of milk & slam the door behind you, you curse under your breath as you take out the garbage

The Story of O tells of love as well, but in a different light

I was standing on a platform in the 14th Street subway station when a guy pointed a gun at me & another guy pressed

a gun against the side of my head & said to my
girlfriend: "What's a chick like you doing with this
faggot?"

The people in the cars wave at me as I walk across the bridge

I see myself crossing the bridge, I'm going back the way
I came

It's too late for me, but maybe you can learn from my experience

She knew I was coming home some day, but she didn't know
exactly when

There was a chain on the door but she didn't hear me when I
called her name

You can't call him a "bachelor" or a "sadist" & expect me
to know what it's like

The blue of the Gitames pack on the table in the stranger's
apartment

Back in the village, in the presence of their weeping sisters,
the Marines were humiliated by their instructors

I look up words in the Thesaurus to make my poems sound more
interesting

He was fired on Tuesday, without notice, & we never saw him
again

Saw an apartment on 13th Street, between 1st & A, three small
rooms for $800. but didn't take it

PICTURES

Something the tenses reveal
as they return to themselves
a hole to be filled
with perfect thoughts
a rent in the fabric
where repression rests
a patch over the place
where the rent appears
not a hole but a wedge
of which I can only say

that once I loved
the light on the hillside
across the lake
& once I heard the cars going by
on the Panhandle
& once I listened to her step
on the stair
& once I lunched in my chair, alone,
while the fan droned on.